This Book Belongs To:

_____

1-2-3...Breathe!

by
Dr. Michelle A. Gramling

You Are Amazing!
Dr. Gramling

Dedication:

To my family and friends,
thank you for your love and support.
My son, Javel, who is my pride and joy.
And in loving memory of Mrs. Sheryl Milton.

1-2-3... Breathe!
Copyright © 2021 by Michelle A. Gramling
Published by: L.I.F.E. with Dr. G
Cover & Interior Design: TamikaINK.com

All rights reserved. No part of this book may be reproduced or transmitted in any form or by any means without written permission from the author.

ISBN-13: 9798700701563

Printed in USA

When your brother or sister gets on your nerves...

When you are frustrated...

When your feelings get hurt...

Everything will be ok, you will see!

THE END

ABOUT THE AUTHOR

Dr. Michelle A. Gramling was born in Columbia, SC but due to her father's military career, she grew up in Europe. She is a licensed clinical social worker and serves as an officer in the United States Air Force. Prior to the military, Dr. Gramling was an elementary school teacher. Through her L.I.F.E. with Dr. G (Living Intentionally, Fully, & Exceptionally) initiative, she aims to plant seeds of positivity in the lives of others. Dr. Gramling enjoys traveling and spending time with family and friends. She is the proud mother of Javel, and auntie to a host of nieces and nephews.

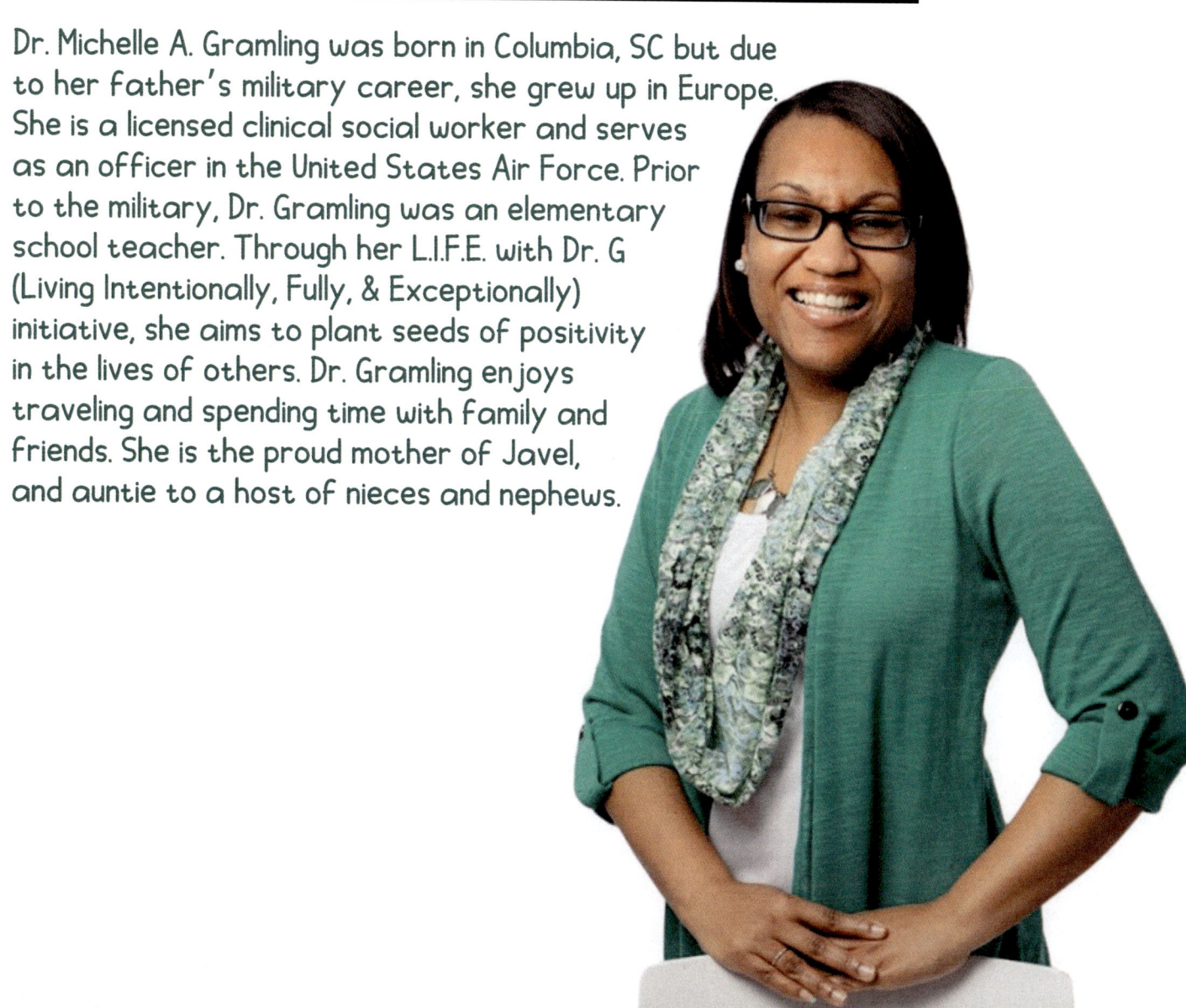

Made in the USA
Monee, IL
26 April 2021